LifeCaps Presents:

Disney's Nine Old Men:

A History of the Animators Who Defined Disney Animation

By Fergus Mason

BookCaps™ Study Guides

www.bookcaps.com

© 2014. All Rights Reserved.

FERGUS MASON

Disney's Nine Old Men

Table of Contents

ABOUT LIFECAPS

LifeCaps is an imprint of BookCaps™ Study Guides. With each book, a lesser known or sometimes forgotten life is recapped. We publish a wide array of topics (from baseball and music to literature and philosophy), so check our growing catalogue regularly (www.bookcaps.com) to see our newest books.

Disney's Nine Old Men

INTRODUCTION

Today, the Walt Disney Company is a huge media conglomerate with a whole range of interests, taking in music labels, cable and network TV, publishing, merchandising and a chain of theme parks in multiple countries. However, it remains best known for its animated films, both short segments and full-length features, and the array of popular characters that star in them. Mickey Mouse, Pluto, Donald Duck, Chip 'n' Dale and many more have entertained children for generations. Hundreds of millions of people worldwide have enjoyed Disney movies like *Snow White and the Seven Dwarves*, *Bambi* and *One Hundred and One Dalmatians*.

Walt Disney founded his media empire as an animation studio in 1923, one of several attempts to set himself up in business as an animator. It was the early days of the industry, and the new studio faced many challenges: staff changes, stiff competition from the likes of Warner Brothers, the Great Depression and complex, often temperamental equipment. Over the next few years many rivals went bankrupt, and there were times when Disney Studios looked like it might follow them down – but that didn't happen. Slowly, the company became one of the leading animation studios in the United States, and then in the world. Then, by releasing the first full-length animated movie, Disney catapulted itself right to the top of the business, a place it held onto decade after decade.

Disney Studios and the films it's produced are intimately associated with one man, Walt Disney himself, but of course there's a lot more to the story than that. Disney had vision and he was willing to work hard, but even producing a ten-minute animated short film is far too much work for any one person. To achieve success, he needed a skilled, dedicated team and Disney knew that. In the beginning there were himself, his brother and a few friends from his previous jobs; soon he was hiring dozens of artists, cameramen and other specialists to work on his projects. By the early 1930s, the Disney Company had hundreds of employees, scores of them directly involved in animation. Among these, though, a small group stood out and went on to make a huge contribution to the golden years of Disney animation.

Starting in 1927, but mostly between 1933 and the beginning of 1935, Disney hired nine young men to work as animation artists. They came from various backgrounds and several different states. Some were professionally trained artists, others had taught themselves through curiosity and hard work. They all had one thing in common though: they were masters at the art of turning a series of drawings into smoothly animated footage and giving it a unique appeal.

When these men went to work for Disney they were mostly in their early to mid-twenties, fresh from college or fired with determination to do something more exciting than illustrating newspaper ads. For the next four decades, they would dominate the studio's animation department, moving up to direct and produce films, and finally training new generations of young artists in how to produce the characteristic Disney look. All of them dedicated their entire careers to the studio and helped make it the leading studio it still is today. For most of those long careers, they carried a name that Walt Disney had jokingly picked up from a book about the Supreme Court way back in 1937. He called them The Nine Old Men.

CHAPTER 1: THE

BEGINNINGS OF DISNEY

Animated movies have a long history in the USA. The first stop-motion films were developed from the techniques used in older devices like the zoetrope, a spinning cylinder with slots down the sides through which a series of images could be seen. Early movies used blackboard drawings, which were changed slightly between shots so that when the film was played at normal speed, the image seemed to move. By 1908, Émile Cohl was drawing images on paper to make cartoons and within another decade the classic cel animation process, which combined multiple transparent sheets to give an image, had been invented. Early characters like Felix the cat were hugely popular, and short animations became a regular feature of a trip to the movies. The animation industry began to expand, and although most studios didn't survive very long, there was a steady stream of ambitious young hopefuls willing to give it a shot. The most famous, of course, was Walt Disney.

Walter Elias Disney was born in Chicago on December 5, 1901. When he was four his family moved to a farm in Missouri for four years, where Walt began to develop an interest in drawing. Next they headed to Kansas City where a school friend introduced him to the theater and movies. He signed up for weekend classes at the Kansas City Art Institute and also enjoyed taking his young sister to a local amusement park.

By the time the Disney family moved back to Chicago in 1917, Walt was a talented artist. He became the cartoonist for his school newspaper, and when the United States entered the First World War, Walt turned his skills to drawing patriotic cartoons. That wasn't enough for him though, so he dropped out of high school and tried to join the army. That was an ambitious plan, but it failed; the recruiters saw through his scheme and rejected him for being underage. Undeterred, he and a friend volunteered for the Red Cross instead. They accepted him, and, although he missed the war itself, he drove an ambulance in France in late 1918.

When he returned to the U.S., Walt had a few ideas for his future career, but he quickly ran into problems. He was a high school dropout in a competitive job market, and nobody wanted to hire him. As a last resort, there was always the jelly factory his father was part owner of but Walt wanted to make his own way in the world. Finally, his brother introduced him to the Pesmen-Rubin Art Studio, who took him on as an illustrator. It was just a temporary job, and the studio was basically an ad agency – Walt spent his days drawing pictures for commercials – but it was about to launch his career.

Ubbe Iwerks was born in Kansas City,Missouri in March 1901, the son of North German immigrants. By 1919, he was drawing cartoons for anyone who'd give him a job, and, like Walt, he managed to get a temporary position with Pesmen-Rubin. The two young illustrators quickly became friends, and when Pesmen-Rubin went out of business in 1920 they decided to set up their own studio. They considered calling it Disney-Iwerks but decided that sounded too much like an eyeglass factory, so finally they settled on Iwerks-Disney Studio Commercial Artists.[1]

Walt and Ubbe (who later shortened his name to Ub) were both highly talented artists, but they were also both very young – just nineteen – and didn't have the experience or contacts to bring in enough business. To help make ends meet, Walt took a job with the Kansas City Slide Company, painting illustrations for movie theater advertisements. Iwerks soon struggled with looking after the company on his own and moved to the Slide Company as well, winding up Disney's first attempt at running his own studio. The company had barely lasted a month from start to finish.

Kansas City Slide Company was in the advertising business, but they also had a lot of connections with the movie industry they serviced and were experimenting with animation. Walt Disney wasn't familiar with animations, but when he first saw one he was fascinated. He started learning everything he could about the technology and realized that, as a skilled cartoonist, this was something he could do himself. In 1921, he was given a chance to prove it. Cartoonist Milton Feld asked him to animate *Newman's Laugh-O-Grams*, a series of twelve cartoons.

After two years with the Slide Company, Walt resigned and took another shot at setting up his own business. This time it was an animation studio, which he named Laugh-O-Gram Films after the movies he'd been hired to make. Using the remaining assets from Iwerks-Disney and $15,000 borrowed from investors he bought a building to use as a studio and hired Iwerks as chief animator. Other members of the team he assembled went on to create some of the most famous cartoon characters of all time – Bugs Bunny, Sylvester and Tweety, Yosemite Sam and more – but this was the early days of the industry and they were still finding out what worked. Altogether they managed to make nine of Feld's twelve films. The first of them was *Alice's Wonderland*, which combined live action and animation. It featured a young girl, played in live action by Virginia Davis, and a variety of cartoon characters. It was never released to movie theaters but formed one of the foundations for Disney's later success.

What it didn't do was bring in a lot of money, and six months after setting up the studio Disney was so broke that he was living in his office and taking weekly baths in the washroom at Union Station. *Alice's Wonderland* was financed with $500 Walt earned from making a film about dental hygiene for Missouri schoolchildren. By July 1923, the studio was bankrupt. Walt paid off all the creditors he could, and then sold his movie camera. He spent the money on a one-way train ticket to Los Angeles.

Disney didn't have much to take to Hollywood with him, but he did have an unfinished reel of *Alice's Wonderland*. With some help from his brother Roy, who'd given up his bank job to join him in California, he managed to scrape together the money to open a new animation studio. Next he sent a copy of *Alice's Wonderland* to Margaret Winkler, a New York movie distributor. Winkler had already made a name for herself in the animation industry by backing the *Felix the Cat* cartoons, and if Walt could get her support he would earn at least enough breathing space to give his new studio a fair chance. He was in luck. Winkler liked what she saw of the concept and wanted a distribution deal for a series based on it.

That left Disney with a studio and financial backing, but no staff. He quickly persuaded Virginia Davis's family to relocate to Hollywood, and Ub Iwerks soon followed. By early 1924, there were enough of them to start work, and over the next three years they made 56 short films, now known as the Alice Comedies. Davis starred in the first thirteen, and the role of Alice was also played by Dawn Paris, Margie Gay and Lois Hardwick. Paris went on to have a reasonably successful career as an actress under the names Anne Shirley and Dawn O'Day, but as the Alice Comedies progressed the role of the live actors gradually faded, and the animated characters became more prominent.

In 1927 Winkler's new husband Charles Mintz ordered a series of films from Disney Brothers Studios. These were to be all-animated, with no live action, and featured a new character called Oswald the Lucky Rabbit. They were distributed through Universal and after a slightly rocky start became hugely popular. The sudden flow of cash allowed Disney to rehire most of his old team from Kansas City. It didn't last – after six months Mintz managed to hire most of the animators out from under Disney and, as he owned the trademark on the character, started to produce the films himself – but it was enough that for the first time the studio was financially secure. Walt and Iwerks also had plenty of ideas, and they started building a new team to carry them out. That team would propel Walt Disney's studio right to the top of the animation business and keep it there for decades to come. Among its early members was Les Clark, who would become the first of the Nine Old Men.

CHAPTER 2: LES CLARK

Leslie James Clark was born in Ogden, Utah on November 17, 1907. Ogden was founded by fur trader Miles Goodyear in 1846; he built a fort near a river junction and ran it as a trading post. A year later, Mormon settlers bought the fort from him and named the settlement Brownsville, but changed the name to Ogden when it was incorporated as a town in 1851. For the next couple of decades it was a small farming community, but the growth of the transport network was about to change that. In 1863, three railway companies began building a line that would span the entire North American continent. It was a huge task; the main US railway network only extended as far west as Council Bluffs, Iowa, and the goal was a line that ended on the shores of San Francisco Bay. The Union Pacific Railroad Company began extending their line west while the Western Pacific and Central Pacific railroads started with their short line from Oakland to Sacramento and began laying track east towards Utah. On May 10, 1869 the "golden spike" was driven into the line at Promontory Summit, 35 miles northwest of Ogden. The new line connected Ogden to both coasts of the USA and spurred a surge of growth that soon made it the second largest city in Utah. It also made it easy for Ogdenites to move on if they felt the urge for somewhere new, and in the early 20th century California was an attractive destination. Les Clark's parents were among many who made the decision to move to Los Angeles.

By 1925, Les was studying at Venice High School, just a few miles from the Disney Brothers Studio in Hollywood. To top up his allowance he also worked part time in a local candy store. He hadn't shown any interest in art until that point and wasn't studying it as a main subject – he probably had to do the usual classes at school, but nothing more than that – and didn't have any ambition to follow an artistic career. Then one day, Walt Disney stopped by the candy store and saw the young man painting decorative lettering on a display mirror. Impressed, Disney complimented him on the good job he was doing.

Les knew who the customer was; the Alice Comedies were a big hit by that point and Disney was becoming well known around Hollywood and the surrounding area. The incident impressed him enough to get him thinking about the future. Les graduated from high school in February 1927. Days later, on February 23, he approached Disney and asked him if he could have a job. Disney asked him to do some test drawings and Les obliged. He worked quickly and confidently, and now it was Disney's turn to be impressed.[2] He hired Les straight away, although he did warn him the job might turn out to be temporary – memories of how his last two studios had failed probably weren't far from his mind.

It was his drawing that had won Les a place at Disney Studios, but it was awhile before he got to do any. In the early days of Disney they were always shorthanded, and there were plenty of jobs to be done around the place. One of the most vital was running the animation cameras. Animation is easy with digital technology, but in 1927 it was a complex and intricate process. Disney Studios used the cel technique, which built up images from multiple layers. Elements that didn't change, like the background, would be painted once and used for multiple shots. Then moving elements, like the characters, would be separately placed on the background to build the scene. The technique has a lot of advantages, with the main one being a big saving in the amount of drawing and painting that needs done. Standard elements can be reused many times. It might take a dozen images, each of them slightly different from the one before, to show a character running a single pace. Once they've been done, however, they can be cycled for pace after pace, and reused in different scenes or even different films. The down side is that very precise positioning and photography is needed to produce a smooth animation. To help with the positioning frames were developed that sandwiched the cels (short for celluloids) under a sheet of glass; marks or even pins round the edge of the frame allowed the cels to be positioned exactly. Then the assembled scene had to be photographed.

The cameras were highly specialized and often temperamental. The design was based on a rostrum camera, a type of movie camera used for filming still pictures and objects. In a standard rostrum camera the actual camera can be panned or zoomed around the object to create more interesting shots; the object itself sits on a stationary table. To adapt them for animations, the camera was fixed in position vertically above the table. Then its mechanism was modified. Rostrum cameras, like standard movie cameras, ran a strip of film through the mechanism at high speed while the shutter opened and closed several times a second. Animated cartoons had to be shot on standard strip movie film, so they could be developed and played on a projector, but it could take a minute or two to rearrange the cels between frames. That meant the camera had to advance the film one frame at a time, then stop. The operator would press the trigger, photographing that shot, then advance it one more frame while the compositor set up the next shot. Cameras designed to spin the film reel at a steady speed could be balky when made to advance single frames, so it was a tricky job. Being young and smart, Les got assigned to it, and for six months he worked the big cameras as the team plotted, drew and painted around him. Then, in early 1928, he got his chance at animation.

After losing Oswald the Lucky Rabbit to Universal, Disney had been looking for a new character to replace him. Iwerks sketched a selection of anthropomorphic animals but none of them appealed to Disney. Then he remembered a half-tame mouse that had lived in his office at the old Laugh-O-Gram studio in Kansas City. He suggested a mouse, and Iwerks came up with some concept drawings. Disney approved them and decided to call the character Mortimer Mouse. His wife disagreed; after some discussion they settled on Mickey Mouse.

The first two Mickey films, *Plane Crazy* and *The Gallopin' Gaucho*, failed to find distributors. They were produced in May and June 1928 with Iwerks as lead animator, with other drawings done by Hugh Harman and Rudolf Ising. This was slightly awkward as Harman and Ising had signed on with Charles Mintz; they were still at Disney because Mintz hadn't managed to set his new studio up yet, and Disney was still working on the final Oswald films he'd contracted for. Despite the failure to find a distributor Iwerks and Disney thought Mickey was worth persevering with and, after Harman and Ising left the studio, they started work on a third film, a Buster Keaton parody called *Steamboat Willie*. To help with the drawing Iwerks was assigned four new artists; one of them was Les Clark.

Iwerks was chief animator for the Mickey films, but he didn't draw every frame himself. Working from the storyboards he and Disney had created, he drew the scenery and key elements for each scene. When it came to the characters and other moving objects, however, he only did part of the work. For each sequence of movement Iwerks would draw the extremes of motion and any key poses. These were then arranged in order and passed on to his assistants, who would draw the poses in between the ones Iwerks had done; this was called inbetweening and those who did it were known, with a remarkable lack of imagination, as inbetweeners.

In effect, Les became an apprentice to Iwerks, who taught him what he needed to know – first as an inbetweener, then as an animator in his own right. *Steamboat Willie* was an intensive course in high quality animation; Iwerks managed to get it done in just two months with help from his new team, and Les ended up drawing hundreds of inbetween images of Mickey and the other characters. In addition to teaching him how to progress each frame to create the illusion of movement, it helped him develop the characteristic style of a Disney artist, a style largely invented by Iwerks. It wasn't long before he was given an opportunity to show off what he'd learned.

Animated films so far had all been silent; Mickey, in *Steamboat Willie*, became the first cartoon character to speak, and that was a big contributor to the film's success. Now Disney's new musical director suggested that as well as more Mickey films they make a series based around sound. The new series, Silly Symphonies, launched in August 1929 with *The Skeleton Dance*. Like many of the series, it didn't have a plot; it simply featured four skeletons dancing round a European-style graveyard of the type shown in the increasingly popular horror movies like *Nosferatu*. The inspiration for the film was dark but *Skeleton Dance* itself was whimsical; the skeletons borrow parts of each other to use as instruments and show off popular dances of the time.

Five animators worked on it, including Disney and Iwerks; Les Clark was one of them. He was responsible for one of the most amusing scenes in the film, where one skeleton disconnects another's legs then uses his ribcage as a xylophone.[3]

From there, Clark went on to work on many more of the Silly Symphonies. He also continued to help Iwerks with the Mickey films. His first credit as an animator was for a Mickey title, *The Barn Dance*, although in fact he had worked as an inbetweener on it. Then, in 1930, he suddenly found himself loaded with a bigger responsibility than he'd expected. Iwerks, who was struggling with a very heavy workload and didn't feel he was valued highly enough, had a falling out with Disney and left suddenly to set up his own studio. That left Mickey without a chief animator and Les, who already had plenty of experience in drawing the character, was the obvious choice for the job.

Clark's first Mickey film as chief animator was *The Fire Fighters*, released on June 25, 1930. Now confident in drawing the character Les began to subtly change it to suit his own style, and the details gradually drifted away from how Iwerks had drawn them. Mickey retained his basic shape, including the circular body that was replaced by a more pear-shaped one in 1938 when Fred Moore took over the role, but overall he looked much more like the modern character than the original version. With Les in charge of development Mickey became the most popular cartoon character in the USA. There were occasional pitfalls, of course. One film – *The Barnyard Battle* – managed to get banned in Germany. In it, Mickey has to join an army of mice defending their homes against an invading force of cats. Les drew the cats with the distinctive spiked *Pickelhaube* helmets worn by German cavalry during the First World War, which the country's censors decided was "an affront to the national dignity."[4]

Over the next decade Disney allocated more and more responsibility to him, including the "Sorcerer's Apprentice" sequence in the long film, *Fantasia*. Released in 1940, this was intended to revive the popularity of Mickey, who had been suffering from declining audiences. In 1947, Les was appointed as animation director for *Fun and Fancy Free*, a two-part film featuring a Mickey story and one about a bear named Bongo. This job meant he had to supervise and direct the work of the whole animation team, including producing style templates and reviewing each day's output of cels. It was a major step on the way to becoming a full director, which he achieved in 1955 with *You, The Human Animal*. He went on to direct eighteen more films for Disney, plus two episodes of the Disneyland TV series. These projects included documentaries and health advice programs as well as films featuring major characters like Donald Duck and Goofy. Among the most popular was the 1958 *Paul Bunyan*.

By the time Les retired from Disney in 1975, he was the longest-serving employee in the company, having been there for 48 years. He died on September 12, 1979, four years after drawing his last cartoon.

CHAPTER 3: ERIC LARSON

In the six years after Les Clark joined Disney the studio grew slowly, producing a steady stream of Mickey cartoons and the Silly Symphonies. Animators came and went, but apart from the departure of Ub Iwerks in 1930 the core team remained. It was 1933 before the next of the Old Men joined the company.

Like Clark, Eric Cleon Larson was a native of Utah; he was born in Cleveland, a hundred miles south of Salt Lake City, on September 3, 1905. Cleveland was very different from Ogden. Established in 1884 as a farmstead, it attracted a few more families and by 1905 had a population of around 450, about the same as it has now. It was and is a small but prosperous farming community and Larson grew up on a farm. As a child he went to Cleveland Elementary School, then to Emory County High School in nearby Castle Dale. In his spare time he read voraciously and developed an interest in satirical magazines. His favorites were the American weekly *Judge* and the classic British *Punch*, the magazine that first used the word "cartoon" to mean a comic drawing. Both magazines were illustrated by famously talented cartoonists and Larson loved the drawings; he began attempting to draw his own, and quickly developed a talent for it.

After graduating from high school in 1925, Larson went to the University of Utah in Salt Lake City where he majored in journalism.[5] His choice of degree made him a natural for the campus newspaper, the *Daily Utah Chronicle*. The *Chronicle* has been running since 1890 and is one of the USA's leading student-run newspapers; it's regularly nominated for awards by the Society of Professional Journalists, and many of its student staff go on to press careers at the state level. It wasn't long before Larson was editing it, as well as contributing his own material. He specialized in humorous pieces and quickly built up a reputation both on and off campus. He was still drawing cartoons too, but not for the student paper; these were published in the *Deseret News*, Utah's oldest paper. The *Deseret News* was also the second most popular paper in the state after *The Salt Lake Tribune*, so Larson's drawings were getting a wide audience.

With his journalism degree in his pocket, Larson had a few options. There wasn't much demand for reporters at home in Cleveland, but he already had contacts with the *Deseret News* and could probably have found himself a job in Salt Lake City easily enough. He'd spent his whole life so far in Utah, though, and he fancied a change. Instead of looking for a place at a local paper he set off around the country, offering his services as a freelance writer along the way. He had the talent and experience to support himself doing that, and along the way he learned a lot more about the business of journalism. It was a bad time to be looking for a permanent job, with the Great Depression in full swing and US unemployment at an all-time high, so he didn't settle down anywhere. Then, in 1933, he reached Los Angeles. He still didn't find a full-time job on a paper; instead he ended up writing for KHJ Radio.

Nowadays KHJ is a Spanish-language station, broadcasting under the name *La Ranchera*, but it only made the language switch in 1989. It started out as a general entertainment station in 1922, and quickly came under the ownership of the *LA Times* group. By the late 1930s, it was the LA affiliate of the recently founded CBS network and handled most of the network's production for the west coast. Bing Crosby's first national radio show was run from KHJ in 1931. The station also broadcast a lot of radio dramas and they were always looking for talented writers.

The first play written specifically for radio was transmitted by Pittsburgh's KDKA in 1921, and within a couple of years the format was being tried out in Britain, in France and across the USA. It was in America that most of the experimentation happened, though; the BBC and most European broadcasters preferred to concentrate on adapting traditional stage plays. Sometimes these worked well, but sometimes they flopped; radio was a very different medium to a theater. If a work was written with broadcasting in mind, it was much more likely to succeed. There were also other possibilities opening up and radio studios were quick to identify them. One of the most interesting was the idea of serials, continuing stories with weekly or even daily episodes. The longest running radio serial in the world is the BBC's *The Archers*, which as of early 2014 has gone through nearly 17,000 episodes, but it's a latecomer that only started in 1950. US networks and even individual stations had been producing dozens of popular serials for decades. Many of these ran for years; others played for one short season. The radio drama sector was growing swiftly

– until television arrived in the 1940s, radio was one of the biggest forms of entertainment in America – and stations were experimenting to see what audiences liked.

Los Angeles was one of the key centers of the radio industry, just as it was for movies, and Eric Larson had the chance to listen to a lot of serials. Not long after arriving in the city he decided he could write one himself, and came up with a plot. KHJ were interested in the idea, titled *The Trail of the Viking*, and hired Eric to write it. He kept drawing cartoons in his spare time though, and one of his friends had an idea. Pointing out how good the drawings were, he persuaded Eric to send some of them to Walt Disney. Disney was impressed and immediately offered him a job as an assistant animator. Eric accepted, abandoning any remaining plans for a career in journalism and moving across to the growing animation industry.

Larson managed to avoid spending time on the animation cameras; the studio had grown enough by then that there wasn't a shortage of support staff. Instead, he got straight to work on drawing animations. Like Clark he started out as an inbetweener, working under Hamilton Luske. Ham Luske had joined the studio two years earlier, already an experienced animator, and quickly earned enough of Disney's trust to be assigned to major projects. His own experience helped him recognize Larson's talent, and before long he promoted him to assistant animator. As Iwerks had done for Clark, Luske mentored the young man and taught him the Disney way of doing things. Within a year he was chosen to work on Disney's most ambitions animation project yet.

Up to now all animated films had been short, with average lengths of less than ten minutes; most of the Mickey Mouse films had been seven to eight minutes long. Disney believed there was a market for full length animated feature films, though, and he was determined to make one. In 1934 he began planning it; by June he was confident enough in the idea to announce it to the *New York Times*. His wife and his brother Roy were less convinced, and repeatedly tried to talk him out of it; the media were scornful of the whole project and leading figures in Hollywood called it "Disney's Folly." Disaster was predicted everywhere. Disney even had to mortgage his house at one point to help fund the production, which finally cost just short of $1.5 million. That was a very high budget for the time, especially for an animated film. MGM's classic *Captains Courageous*, which was in production at the same time, cost $1.6 million, but that included fees for a long list of top actors, including Spencer Tracy, Lionel Barrymore and Mickey Rooney. Disney's project needed only voice actors and animators – lots of animators. The finished film ran for 83 minutes with 24 frames per second, almost 120,000 frames in total. Unlike a typical short, there were dozens of scenes and dozens of characters; even using the cel process there was an immense amount of drawing to be done. Ham Luske felt that Larson was now experienced enough to contribute, and he was appointed to the project as a full animator.

Eric's job on *Snow White* was animating some of the animals, with one of the high points being the "Whistle while you work" sequence. It was the start of a glorious list of jobs on Disney classics; after the success of *Snow White* the studio settled down to release a major new feature every two or three years – barely even pausing for the Second World War – and Eric was involved in almost all of them. He animated dancing marionettes in *Pinocchio*, baby animals in *Dumbo*, and some of the wolves in *The Jungle Book*. He did several of the dogs in *A Hundred and One Dalmatians*, and the barn animals in *Mary Poppins*. Personally, he felt his best work was on *Pinocchio*, and especially the character of Figaro the cat. With Figaro he managed to achieve one of the most difficult tasks for an animator: produce a character that's believable as an animal but also shows credible human emotions.

For *Fantasia*, Eric was promoted to directing animator for the "Pastoral Symphony" segment, but after his satisfaction with *Pinocchio* the new film was a disappointment to him; the centaurs, in particular, were something he regretted for years afterwards. He had the ability to learn from his mistakes, though, and he recognized what he'd done wrong; a four-legged animal was moving like a human. When he went to work on *Bambi* he remembered that, and his work ended up better than ever.

Larson's versatility made him an ideal candidate in 1973 when the company stepped up its efforts to recruit a new generation of animators. Eric was put in charge of finding, attracting and training talented young artists and integrating them into the team to replace the old guard who were retiring. The people he brought in are the directors and senior animators who brought Disney into the 21st century.

In the end, Eric overtook Les Clark's length of service at Disney; when he finally retired in 1986 he had been with the company for 53 years. He died two years later, on October 25, 1988, at his home in La Cañada Flintridge, California.

CHAPTER 4: WOLFGANG REITHERMAN

The first two of the Old Men were both Utah natives. The third came from further afield. Wolfgang Reitherman was born in Munich, Germany on June 26, 1909. In 1911 his family moved to the United States, and like many German immigrants, they ended up in Kansas City, Missouri. By coincidence, the Reitherman's new home was just round the corner from Disney's brother and financial backer, Roy.[6] When Wolfgang was a teenager they moved again, this time joining the growing stream of people heading to California.

California's population was growing rapidly at the time and new industries were moving in. The aerospace industry was one of them, and it caught Wolfgang's attention early on. As he grew up he dreamed of becoming a pilot, and while he was still at high school he started taking flying lessons. Pilot's licenses weren't required at the time and as long as the sixteen-year-old Wolfgang could pay for fuel and flight time there was nothing to stop him. He admitted to being shaken when friends were killed in flying accidents but it didn't stop him.[7] He then went on to study technical drawing at Pasadena Junior College; when he graduated from there he went looking for a job with an aviation company, and Santa Monica-based Douglas Aircraft took him on as a draftsman. Douglas was a fast-growing business at the time, and had ambitions of capturing a large share of the growing airline market. In the early 1930s they were working on their prototype DC-1 airliner, which would eventually evolve into the famous DC-3 Dakota and the military C-47 transport. It was a busy time in their drawing shops, and for Wolfgang it was a high-intensity introduction to the field of aircraft design.

For whatever reason, Reitherman didn't enjoy working at Douglas. It didn't affect his interest in flying but drawing aircraft parts, he decided, was not for him. Drawing in general seems to have in-

terested him more, though, because on leaving
Douglas he enrolled at the Chouinard Art Institute.

The Chouinard Art Institute was founded as a private art school in 1921 by artist and educator Nelbert Murphy Chouinard. Born in Minnesota,
Chouinard had studied art at Brooklyn's Pratt Institute before moving to California. Later, she decided
that the West Coast needed its own school of fine
arts and, not being one to hang around waiting, she
set one up. Her school went on to develop close
links with Disney; in 1961, Walt and Roy helped
arrange a merger with the Los Angeles Conservato-
ry of Music, creating the California Institute of the
Arts. In 1932, when Reitherman enrolled, it was a
lively and varied school located in a modern art
deco building on South Grand View, LA. Nelbert
Chouinard was a progressive who believed that
commercial illustrators needed the same skills and
mindset as traditional artists, so the school offered
a wide range of classes; by the late 1930s it even had
specialized facilities for training animators. Wolfgang had decided to become a watercolor artist so
he was concentrating on sketching and composition. He wasn't a great student, however, because he
spent so much time working on his own sketches
and paintings instead of his set works for the
course. Becoming an animator had never crossed
his mind.

Walt Disney thought about little else but animators, though, and as well as looking for new ones,
he was always trying to hone the skills of the ones
he already had. In 1933, he invited Don Graham, a
teacher at the Chouinard School, to run evening
classes for the studio's animators.[8] Graham was
happy to do it, and soon got to know the animators
and how they worked. Then, back at Chouinard, he
noticed Wolfgang's sketches. Something about their
style convinced him the young man had the talent
to do animations, and he managed to arrange an
introduction to Walt Disney. Walt liked the sketches too, and immediately offered Wolfgang a job at
the studio. Wolfgang himself wasn't sure, though.
He enjoyed sketching, but wasn't sure how much
fun it would be drawing basically the same thing
over and over again. Disney suggested he try it for
a couple of weeks to see how it went. Wolfgang
agreed – and was immediately hooked. He "fell in
love with movement," he said.

Like most Disney animators at the time, his first
task was one of the Silly Symphonies. *Funny Little
Bunnies*, released just before Easter 1934, didn't feature any continuing Disney characters. Instead it
showed rabbits making a variety of Easter treats,
including chocolate eggs and painted boiled ones,
with the assistance of chickens and other birds.
Even now it's one of the most popular Silly Symphonies. It also gave Reitherman a flying start to

his Disney career; he was soon assigned to more Symphonies and then to Mickey films. One of the best known of these was *Hawaiian Holiday*, where he animated the scenes of Goofy attempting to surf.

When animation started on *Snow White and the Seven Dwarves*, Wolfgang found himself on the project and was given an entire scene to produce himself. It featured the dwarves making an elaborate four-poster bed for Snow White and Disney admired the technique that had gone into it. At the same time he had second thoughts about the scene itself; he was worried that the pace of the film was too slow, and was looking for scenes to cut. In the end the bed-making scene was one of them. His other project for the film, the magic mirror, was luckier and survived to the final version.

When *Snow White* became a huge success and Disney went on to make his next full length feature, *Pinocchio*, Wolfgang was one of the animators picked for the film. Some of his work on *Snow White* might never have made it into the final release, but it had impressed Disney enough for him to give Reitherman one of the key sequences.

The most dramatic villain in *Pinocchio* is Monstro, the enormous whale who ends up swallowing both Pinocchio and his creator Geppetto; then, after they escape by making him sneeze, pursues them. The chase scene is still regarded by experts as one of the most dramatic pieces of animation ever; Disney wanted it to be one of the centerpieces of the film and he entrusted it to Reitherman. The results lived up to his expectations, and although the scene never earned the public acclaim Disney (and Reitherman) thought it deserved, it was enough to cement his reputation as one of the studio's most talented animators.

Pinocchio was released in February 1940; *Fantasia* followed in November. Although it was feature length film, *Fantasia* wasn't a single story like the previous two films, but a collection of eight separate segments with classical music accompaniment; the most famous is probably Mickey's *Sorcerer's Apprentice* scene, but one that caused a lot of comment at the time was a fight to the death between a triceratops and a tyrannosaurus rex. The sequence was Wolfgang's work, and it was the first animated film of dinosaurs ever made.

Reitherman also worked on Disney's next three features, *The Reluctant Dragon*, *Dumbo* and *Saludos Amigos*. The last of these was released in August 1942, and it was to be his last project for several years. The USA had entered the Second World War in December 1941 and Reitherman, with his long interest in flying, joined the United States Army Air Force.

In war, it's the fighter pilots who get most of the glory, but as soldiers often say, "Amateurs talk tactics, professionals talk logistics." Modern armed forces can't operate without huge amounts of fuel, ammunition and rations, so without the logistics "tail" the fighting "teeth" soon wither away. Most transport in WWII was done by sea, rail or road, but for the first time transport aircraft also played a vital role. Where there wasn't a road network it was often the only way to deliver supplies to fighting units. Wolfgang Reitherman trained as a transport pilot and played his part in hauling stores around. It might be an unglamorous job but it can also be a dangerous one; the weather and terrain are a constant hazard, as well as enemy aircraft. In 1943, the British began launching raids deep behind Japanese lines in Burma, using the "Chindits" – a special forces unit made up of British and Gurkha troops. The US Army quickly copied the idea and set up "Merrill's Marauders." These forces had around 3,000 troops each and they moved through the jungle on foot in columns of several hundred men. Although each soldier carried up to half his own body weight in food, water and ammunition, they still needed constant resupply; an experiment by Merrill in operating without support nearly led to disaster as malnutrition weakened his men. The Chindits were initially supported by the Indian Air Force (which was part of the Royal Air Force at the time) but as Merrill's Marauders prepared to go into action the USAAF volunteered to help. First Air Commando was set up for the job, operating a mix of gliders, C-47s and light transport aircraft. Most supplies were dropped from C-47s by parachute to be collected by the roving Chindit columns, but the smaller aircraft also had a vital role. L-1 and L-5 planes, along with six experimental helicopters, could land on small airstrips hacked out of the jungle to evacuate casualties. For small or fragile cargos, UC-64 Norseman light transports could also land in the jungle, and Reitherman flew one of these. It was no job for a nervous man, weaving through the high mountain ranges to put down on a tiny, rough jungle airstrip, but Reitherman excelled at it. By the end of the war, he had been promoted to Major and awarded the Distinguished Flying Cross. He also met his future wife in 1946, towards the end of his service, while she was working as an air stewardess on a transport flight to the Philippines.[9]

On leaving the Air Force in 1947, Wolfgang immediately asked Disney for his old job back, and of course he got it. Straight away he was back to work, animating on *Fun and Fancy Free*. He continued to work as an animator on every Disney feature for the next twelve years, until 1959's *Sleeping Beauty*, which he also directed. From then on he directed many of Disney's most famous films, including *101 Dalmations*, *The Jungle Book* and *The Rescuers*. He was well known in the studio for taking on action scenes that other artists were intimidated by, but which he loved drawing, and for using his own experiences to improve animations; the flight scenes in *The Rescuers*, although they featured mice flying on the back of Orville the albatross, were planned using his knowledge of transport aircraft to blend realism with the comedy. By 1961, he was Disney's chief animation director; for his last film, 1981's *The Fox and the Hound*, he was the producer.

When Walt Disney died in died in 1966, it was Woolie Reitherman who kept the animation team running. Disney had been the creative driving force behind the studio and it would have been easy for things to fall apart without him, but Reitherman had the leadership ability and vision to step into the gap.[10] He credited this to his service in the Air Force. "When I was flying the main thing was to keep that airplane in the air," he said, "and that was my feeling that this great group of animators – really, the best in the world – needed to stay airborne towards a new objective."

That new objective was to build a more team-focused Disney Studios that was less dependent on the decisions of one man, and Reitherman succeeded in shepherding the studio that way. From Disney's death until his own retirement in 1981, he was one of the leading figures in Disney's management and deserves a lot of the credit for how well the company survived the loss of its founder.

Reitherman himself died on May 22, 1985 in a car accident near his home in Burbank, California.

CHAPTER 5: FRANK THOMAS

Many of the junior animators and support staff at Disney were from Los Angeles and the surrounding area, but Frank Thomas was the first California native among the Old Men. Born in Fresno on September 5, 1912 Franklin Rosborough Thomas wanted to be a professional artist from the age of nine; he remembered asking his father, who was the president of Fresno State College, how to make money drawing pictures.[11] He was a quiet boy and preferred to spend time reading and drawing, but he wasn't antisocial; he could and did make friends. When he graduated high school and started studying at Fresno State, he quickly became a popular student, and a talented one. He was at Fresno State for two years, and in between he went to summer school at the University of Southern California in Los Angeles. While there he became interested in film, and in his second year at Fresno State he started building up some practical experience. With some fellow students he wrote and produced a movie as a class project; it was a spoof based on student life, and it was good enough to be played in local theaters.

Frank's father was a great believer in education, being an educator himself, but he also felt it was important for people to do what they enjoyed. Seeing how keen his son was on the movie industry he offered a deal; if Frank finished his college degree, he would pay for him to study for two years at any art school he chose.[12]

Frank did indeed finish his degree, moving from Fresno State College to Stanford University for his final two years. While at Stanford he got involved in the university's humorous magazine, the *Stanford Chaparral*. This publication, affectionately known as the *Chappie*, has been continuously in print longer than any other humor magazine in the USA and worldwide, only the Swiss *Nebelspalter* has been running longer. Many prominent cartoonists, authors, performers and movie personalities have worked for it as students, and despite being a campus magazine it's nationally distributed. While drawing for the *Chappie* Frank befriended another magazine student staffer, Ollie Johnston; this would be a lifelong friendship. Other friends he made through the *Chappie* were Thor Putnam and Jim Alger.

When he graduated from Stanford, Frank's father kept his word and paid for him to go to art school. Frank's choice, even if he didn't know it at the time, would take him one step closer to Disney; he decided to go to the Chouinard Art Institute. It wasn't long before Putnam and Ollie joined him there.

At Chouinard Frank studied to be an illustrator, but struggled with it – or at least believed he did. One thing that struck people about Frank, through his whole life, was his low opinion of his own talent. He'd started drawing because his older brother enjoyed it, but he never had much faith in his own abilities. What he did have was the determination to improve, and he worked very hard to overcome what he saw as his lack of natural talent. Part of his effort to do that was to sign up for some extra drawing classes with Don Graham, the tutor who ran the classes at Disney.

Don Graham had encouraged Wolfgang Reitherman to apply to Disney, but Frank Thomas made the decision himself. He was spurred on by two of his Stanford friends, Jim Algar and Thor Putman. In summer 1934 they started working at the Disney studio, Algar as an animator, Putman as a layout artist. Frank was keen to join them and, despite his lack of confidence, figured he might as well apply for a job too. He was right; on September 24 he was hired as an animator.

Frank started as an inbetweener. By this time, the studio had grown and become better organized, and there was a system for allocating junior animators to tasks. Inbetweeners were pooled, and animators would go to the pool when they needed work done. He worked in the pool for six months, assisting on Mickey Mouse films and Silly Symphonies. It wasn't long before one of the senior animators began to mentor him, as often happened at Disney; in Frank's case it was Fred Moore. Moore's intervention couldn't have come at a better time, because the supervisor of the pool had taken a dislike to Frank. The supervisor, George Drake, wasn't well liked by the animators as he had no artistic talent himself – it was widely believed that he only managed to get a job at Disney because he was married to *Snow White* director Ben Sharpsteen's sister.[13] He seems to have been intent on finding a way to get Frank fired, but Moore's intervention made that impossible; Fred was a key animator on *Snow White*, which had to succeed or the studio would be bankrupted, and Drake had enough sense not to upset him.

Disney was continuing his efforts to improve the team, and now he had Don Graham running a series of compulsory after-hours classes. These included sessions on movement and "action analysis," to help the animators get a better understanding of how people and animals move. They watched old films and learned movie-making techniques. Frank thought it was great, and he quickly started putting the lessons into his work. It wasn't long before he was given his own tasks on Mickey films – his first project as an assistant animator was a scene in *Mickey's Circus* – and then Moore brought him onto the *Snow White* team. He was one of eight animators who worked on the dwarves and quickly became one of the most productive in that group; he's been given credit for the way his drawings helped give each dwarf a distinct personality.

After his successful work on *Snow White* Frank was chosen to work on several more features over the next few years. His projects included *Fantasia* and *Dumbo*. In 1941 he joined Disney on a tour of South America, which helped to inspire two Latin-themed films: *Saludos Amigos* and *The Three Caballeros*. Then the USA joined the war and he was drafted. Like Reitherman, he ended up in the Air Force, but as a non-pilot his military career was very different.

Walt Disney had channeled most of the profits from *Snow White* into building a large new studio in Burbank, where the company remains today. It was one of the newest and best equipped movie studios in the country and had obvious uses for producing propaganda. Disney offered to work for the war effort in an effort to keep as many of his team together as possible, and was soon hired to produce public information and motivational films for the US and Canadian governments. The armed forces had their own film units, though, and the animators they'd already drafted were quickly posted into them. Frank found himself in the USAAF's First Motion Picture Unit.

The First Motion Picture Unit was set up in July 1942 and immediately began recruiting from the movie industry. Its commander was Jack Warner, head of Warner Brothers, who, despite having no military experience was abruptly commissioned as a Lieutenant Colonel in the US Army. Warner could bring in talent from both civilian and military actors: Clark Gable worked with the unit, and Warner's personnel officer (and later Adjutant) was Captain Ronald Reagan. Through the rest of the war it produced over 400 films, both documentaries for the public like the classic *Memphis Belle: A Story of a Flying Fortress* and military training films. Many of them were live action; others were animations. One of the best known of these was *Camouflage*, in which Yehudi the chameleon explains the principles of camouflage and concealment. It was a twenty-minute animation featuring original characters, it's still seen as a classic of basic fieldcraft training, and it was Frank Thomas's work. During production, he worked with military researchers who were working on advanced camouflage techniques. One of them involved mounting lights on submarine-hunting bombers to match their average brightness to the sky and hide their distinctive silhouettes; perhaps inspired by Frank's elusive reptilian disguise expert, the Navy named them Yehudi Lights.

Reitherman flew in North Africa, China, Burma, India and the South Pacific. Frank's war was a lot closer to home; their first base was at the Warner Brothers studio in Burbank, not far from Disney. Later they moved to Vitagraph Studios in Hollywood, but that location hadn't been maintained and wasn't up to the standard they needed. Finally they took over Hal Roach Studios in Culver City – the home of the *Laurel and Hardy* films – and informally renamed it Fort Roach. Frank got to spend the whole war within fifteen miles of his old job but that didn't reduce his contribution to the campaign; his animations helped teach hundreds of thousands of servicemen the skills they needed to survive and win. He unit earned its motto, "We kill 'em with fil'm."

First Motion Picture Unit disbanded in December 1945 and Frank was discharged from the USAAF a month later. After demobilization leave he went straight back to Disney, who rehired him on April 1, 1946.[14] He went on to animate for all the classic Disney features of the next 30 years, specializing (but not exclusively) in animal characters. He created the spaghetti-eating scene from *Lady and the Tramp*, the monkey chief King Louie from *The Jungle Book* (including the classic *I Wanna Be Like You* song sequence) and the penguin dance in Mary Poppins. He also worked on Disney's controversial adaptations of the *Winnie the Pooh* books, drawing Pooh and Piglet.

By 1950, Frank was senior enough to be chosen as a directing animator and he did that job on several of Disney's best-loved features. His first task in the role was to direct the drawing of the evil stepmother in Cinderella. Later he went on to supervise the Queen of Hearts in *Alice in Wonderland* and the villainous pirate Captain Hook in *Peter Pan*.

Frank wasn't just a talented animator; he could also play the piano, and that got him involved in another Disney group. He was a jazz fan, like many other Disney employees, and some of them came up with a way of livening up their lunch breaks at the studio. They'd set up a record player and the musicians among them would play along. Some of them were professionals; Disney kept in-house musicians to do their soundtracks. Some, like Frank, were enthusiastic amateurs. They all just enjoyed playing along with the music. Then one day, the record player broke. Undaunted, they kept playing. Later they discussed how it had sounded and decided they were good enough to play in public. They started off as the Hugageedy 8, then changed their name to the San Gabriel Valley Blue Flowers. Finally they decided to go along on a trip to San Diego organized by the Horseless Carriage Club. The club had strict rules about only using classic vehicles and at first they had trouble finding something old enough to qualify, but big enough to carry a seven-member band (numbers went up and down). Eventually they found a 1914 fire truck. Pleased with the image they rigged themselves up in fireman's helmets and red shirts, changed their name again to the Firehouse Five Plus Two and set off for San Diego.

The Firehouse Five Plus Two turned out to be the big hit of the tour and soon they were playing at jazz clubs throughout California. Screenwriter Lester Koenig formed a new record label, Good Time Jazz, and signed the band for his first four singles. Through the 1950s and into the 60s they played to huge crowds in Los Angeles, San Francisco and even Las Vegas; they even turned firemen's gear into a fashion item in the Bay Area for awhile.

Professional musicians played with them as guests, and they made friends from the influential New Orleans jazz scene. For a venture that started out as an informal lunch break ensemble, it was a spectacular success.

Frank finally retired from Disney in early 1978, but that wasn't the end of his association with the company. Together with his friend Ollie he wrote Disney's "bible" of animation drawing, *Disney Animation: The Illusion of Life*. He also appeared in a documentary with his friend, titled *Frank and Ollie*. His final involvement in a Disney film was the 2004 movie *The Incredibles*. This was computer animated, as most recent productions have been, but that didn't matter; he was a voice actor this time.

The Incredibles wasn't just Frank's last project for Disney; it was the last major project of his life. He died of a cerebral hemorrhage months later, on September 8, 2004, at home in La Cañada Flintridge.

CHAPTER 6: WARD KIMBALL

Ward Walrath Kimball was born in Minneapolis on March 4, 1914. His mother noticed very early that he was interested in railroads and trains; his first recognizable drawing was of a locomotive.[15] From Ward's accounts of his early life that might have been about the limits of her deductive abilities; he later said, "My mother was just plain dumb."[16] His upbringing was unstable; his father was a businessman whom Ward remembered as being highly intelligent but consistently unsuccessful, and the family moved around a lot and often had financial problems. When he was seven, his parents, tem-

porarily unable to support him, sent him to live
with his grandmother for a year. She nurtured an
interest in drawing, and also exposed him to newspaper cartoon strips which he found fascinating.
Through high school he developed a strong talent
for art and decided he wanted to be a magazine illustrator. Luckily, his art teachers agreed he had the
talent for it, and when he graduated from high
school in 1932 he was offered a scholarship to the
Santa Barbara School of the Arts.[7]

In addition to trains, Kimball was interested in music, and played jazz trombone. In his spare time, he
looked around for musical opportunities, and
quickly found one. Since 1930, Santa Barbara has
been home to the Arlington Theater, built by Fox
studios as a showcase movie theater but also used
for other performing arts. Kimball was already familiar with the Arlington, as he used to go there to
watch cartoons. Now he found there was a children's band based there, and before long he was the
band leader.

Among the cartoons Kimball watched were many
Disney shorts, including the Silly Symphonies. One
that particularly impressed him was *Three Little Pigs*,
released in 1933. Something about the drawing style
appealed to him and he began wondering if, instead
of illustrating magazine stories, he could draw animations instead. One of his instructors encouraged

him, and finally persuaded him to take his portfolio to Disney Studios.

Disney agreed with his instructor's opinion, and Ward was immediately hired. Again, he started off in the inbetweeners pool, where he worked on several shorts including *The Silly Symphony, The Goddess of Spring*. Like Frank Thomas, he didn't get along with George Drake, and he didn't enjoy his time in the pool, but he persevered and it paid off. Like most of his colleagues he found a senior animator to mentor him, Ham Luske. In 1935, he was tasked to draw for *The Tortoise and the Hare*, which won Disney's third Academy Award for best animated short film. The first job where he did his own animation, rather than assisting someone else, was *Elmer Elephant*, but his career really took off with *Woodland Café* in 1936, where he animated a cellist grasshopper that formed part of the café's orchestra. He also worked on *Snow White*, as did almost all of the Old Men – that first feature-length film was a defining event for Disney as an animation studio. Ward's contributions were a scene where the dwarves ate soup and elements of Reitherman's bed-making scene. In the end, neither of these made it into the final cut and Kimball took it badly; he was convinced that the deletions were because Disney didn't think his animation as good enough. In fact, he went to see Disney so he could resign in person. The conversation didn't go quite the way he expected.

Walt Disney later called Kimball a "genius" for the quality of his work. He certainly hadn't been unhappy with his contributions to Snow White; it was all a matter of the film's pace. Now he told Kimball that he was so pleased with his progress he was going to hand him more responsibility for the upcoming Pinocchio. Ward was given the job of designing an important character. Jiminy Cricket, who acts as the voice of Pinocchio's conscience, was one of the most popular characters in the film thanks to Kimball's distinctive approach to animation (and was possibly influenced by his similar 1936 grasshopper character). In addition to designing Jiminy's look, Ward drew most of his scenes, including his speech to Pinocchio, in the pool hall. It was a challenge. Kimball later said that after Snow White the team was overconfident when they started Pinocchio, but quickly ran into trouble because of the difference between relatively realistic human characters and the more stylized ones required for the new story. Jiminy Cricket was particularly difficult; initial concepts weren't cute enough to suit Disney – "He looked like a cockroach," Kimball said[18] – and it was only when Ward came up with his simpler and more anthropomorphic design that Disney was happy with it.

As well as quickly making a mark professionally, Ward also had an active social life at the studio. Outside work he hung around with Fred Moore and storyboard artist Walt Kelly. He also met a girl from the Paint and Ink Department, a busy and vital part of the studio's infrastructure, and struck up a relationship. Her name was Betty Lawyer, and the couple married in 1936.[19]

When war broke out, Kimball was one of the staff who stayed behind at the studio. Instead of drafting him, the government decided he would be more useful playing a role in Disney's war department filmmaking. Many of the staff who stayed on from 1941 to 1945 had only bad memories of the experience; their creativity was seriously limited by the material they were being asked to produce and a lot of them found it gloomy. One of the low points was *Education for Death*, a propaganda short aimed at portraying Nazi Germany as a nation geared purely towards war. Based on a book written by German-American who'd lived in Germany from 1928 until 1939, it tells the story of how a young German boy is brought up to despise weakness then indoctrinated into a Nazi. It ends with the boy – now a young man – marching off with his army comrades then transforming into a row of military graves. For animators used to more cheerful subject matter it was highly depressing. Kimball, though, applied his quirky style to it and found the work highly enjoyable. In one scene, he drew Hitler as an armored knight dancing with Hermann Goering, who he portrayed as a distinctly Wagnerian woman. In fact, Kimball had so much fun with that scene that one of the editors, a man Kimball detested, trimmed it out of fear it would fall victim to indecency laws.

After the war, Kimball continued to build his skills, and became ever more deeply involved in the development and design of characters. He also stayed involved in other aspects of life at Disney. It was Ward who, the day the record player broke, had the idea of turning their informal music group into a jazz band. Through the life of the Firehouse Five Plus Two and its predecessors he was the one who came up with ideas, found them venues to play and shaped their style. He also became famous for his Christmas cards. Every year, starting from 1936, he designed a card to send to family and friends. By the 1960s, he was sending out over a thousand every year, and as December approached, there was always a buzz of anticipation to see what he'd done this time. The style varied far and wide across the field of art, from simple woodcuts to intricate caricatures and almost everything in between. Some of them included photographs of his family, either straight portraits or humorous collages. One was even a photograph of wooden dolls. Photography was another great passion of his life, and sometimes it irked his family. His daughter Kelly recalled how, as she grew older she became self-conscious and didn't like to be photographed, and her father's urge to capture everything on film drove her nuts.[20]

By 1953, Ward had branched out into directing, on top of his animation work. Two of his short films won Academy Awards, and he also directed animation for several features including *Bedknobs and Broomsticks* and *Mary Poppins*. He produced and directed three films on the space program for the *Disneyland* TV show.[21] He also continued an active social life among a wide circle of Disney colleagues. His interest in trains was as strong as ever, and in addition to model railroads the grounds of his home contained a collection of working locomotives. At parties, he would occasionally fire one up on his short private track. He also retained his mischievous sense of humor. When Disney died, Kimball was the originator of the urban legend that he'd had his body cryonically preserved.[22]

Kimball finally retired from Disney in 1974, but kept working on his own projects. He also returned to Disney occasionally for publicity events. He died in Los Angeles on July 8, 2002.

CHAPTER 7: MILT KAHL

Milton Erwin Kahl was born into a family of German immigrants in San Francisco on March 22, 1909. Like Kimball, his background wasn't an affluent one; in fact, his family was very poor, and to make matters worse, his father abandoned them when Milt was young.[23] He was extremely upset and bitter about this; partly to manage his feelings he started drawing on whatever he could find, often just spare pieces of toilet paper. As his skills developed he started scraping together the money to buy proper sketch pads and kept practicing, and soon his ability with a pencil was way ahead of other boys his age. Unfortunately, he didn't get the chance to hone it further with a formal art education, as so many professional animators had done; when he was 16 he had to drop out of high school and look for a job to help support the family.

He got lucky. The Great Depression hadn't begun so there were plenty of laboring jobs available for a teenager with no school qualifications, but Milt found something that suited his talents better. He left school in 1925, and within weeks he landed himself a job with the *Oakland Post Enquirer*, in the art department. He might not have been to art school but his drawing was good enough for the paper to want him as an illustrator. At the *Post Enquirer* he worked with another illustrator who was to play a major part in his later career, Hamilton Luske, who, as an illustrator and later director at Disney would mentor several of the Old Men. For now, Luske, like him, was busy drawing cartoons and ads for a local paper.

After three years at the *Post Enquirer,* Milt found a job at a larger-circulation paper, the *San Francisco Bulletin*. Having gained more experience and also entrusted with more responsibility, his work developed quickly. The timing was wrong, though. As the Depression began to demolish the US economy, the paper's profits started to fall, and Milt was laid off. He didn't give up and soon found himself a job drawing publicity cards for movie theaters. That

was fairly secure; the Depression was a grim time
but the movies stayed surprisingly popular, offering
people a cheap way to forget their problems for a
while, and competition between theaters was in-
tense. They all wanted high quality artwork to draw
in the audiences, and Milt gave them what they
were looking for. Unfortunately, they didn't all give
him what he was looking for, and he had a temper.
One of his perks was free movie tickets, but when
he tried to pass some on to a friend, they were
turned down and he exploded. That cost him his
job, a potential disaster in that tough period. Again
he persevered and again he found something new,
this time in a commercial art studio of the ad
agency Lord & Thomas. In addition to paying the
bills, this gave him more opportunities to perfect
his skills; he was sharing a studio with Fred
Ludekens, one of California's greatest commercial
illustrators. A former fisherman with no art training, Ludekens nevertheless pulled in contracts to
draw and paint for national papers and magazines
as well as producing advertisements and illustrating
books. He had a special genius for drawing animals,
and perhaps seeing the same raw talent in Milt that
he had himself, he coached the younger man in his
techniques. Kahl also invested some of his earnings
in life drawing classes, and by the summer of 1933,
his skills had reached a new peak. As well as his
own grasp of imagery, he'd picked up a lot of

Ludeken's precise, economical style – a style ideally suited to animation, where clear and vivid drawings were essential.

With the economy still suffering, Milt struggled as a commercial artist; he was desperate to find something dependable that would assure him of an income. Then he got lucky. His former colleague, Ham Luske, had started work with Disney in 1931, and now he got in touch. If Milt was interested, Luske said, why not come work for the studio? He certainly was interested, and jumped on a train to Los Angeles. On June 25, 1934 he was hired by the Disney Company.

As usual, Milt started off in the inbetweeners pool. At first he didn't attract much notice; his lack of formal art training, which was no secret in the studio, meant a lot of the illustrators didn't take him seriously. He was also a definite rough diamond, with a vocabulary that wouldn't have been out of place on the docks. Among the mostly college-educated team he was an anomaly. When he was asked to draw, though, his talent was obvious and gradually the more senior animators started to pay attention. The first to take Milt under his wing was Bill Roberts. Although they worked together for a year, they weren't a perfect team; Milt had learned to analyze scenes from Ludeken and his drawings were notable for near-perfect composition, whereas

Roberts tended to just throw himself into tasks without a lot of planning. It was all more experience, however, and for the icing on the cake there were Don Graham's evening classes as well. It all paid off. In his second year with Disney, Ben Sharpsteen asked him to come up with a concept for a few scenes in *Mickey's Circus*. He put together some drawings, and after studying them Sharpsteen, who Milt viewed as a bit of a tyrant[24], told him to do the scenes. *Mickey's Circus* wasn't one of the high points of Disney's 1930s work but Milt's work was good enough to earn him a place on the *Snow White* team.

The tasks he was given for the new feature suited his skills perfectly; he was given several scenes to animate. None of them were key elements of the film, but the way he did them added a lot to the atmosphere; the turtle got particular praise. He was now an established member of the animation team, and when work started on *Pinocchio* it wasn't long before he was brought in.

The title character, Pinocchio himself, was a real problem for the animators. Disney's aim was to stay as close to the original story as he could but something had to be done about the obnoxious, unlikeable puppet. The character from the book was bad enough but the initial sketches for the animations, which emphasized the fact he was a puppet, made things even worse. Kahl suggested – then sketched – an obvious solution: he drew Pinocchio as a much more appealing boy, and then added puppet joints once his appearance was developed. That made the character far more sympathetic. Fred Moore was impressed, and showed the drawings to Ollie Johnston and then to Disney himself; Milt's reward was to be made supervising animator for the character of Pinocchio.[25] It was a perfect choice; his analytical approach to design let him calculate exactly how cute Pinocchio should be to keep his bad behavior through much of the film on the right side of believable.

Realism was a vital component of Milt's next project. Along with Frank Thomas, he missed *Fantasia*; instead he was working on *Bambi*. He started by studying real deer, watching how they moved and endlessly sketching them to capture their proportions. Then he worked out how they had to be altered to animate properly and have the maximum appeal to audiences. Frank Thomas later said that *Bambi* was the best work Kahl had ever done.

It certainly wasn't the last work he ever did though; in fact, it was barely the beginning. For close to 40 years he played key roles in almost everything Disney did; in addition to doing his own share of the animation, he helped refine the final appearance of nearly every main character. The list of characters whose animation he supervised is like a *Who's Who* of Disney's best-loved names: Bambi and Thumper, Alice, Lady and the Tramp, Pongo the Dalmatian and many more. Of course there were characters he didn't get to work on that he'd have loved to do, often the more mischievous ones like the Cheshire Cat. He did get to supervise King Louie in the *Jungle Book*, as well as Shere Khan the tiger and the snake Kaa.

In 1976, Milt retired from Disney Studios and returned to his beloved San Francisco Bay. In retirement, he worked on sculpture and other hobbies, but his legacy at the studio continued. He died of pneumonia at his home in Mill Valley, just across the Golden Gate in Marin County, on April 19, 1987. In 2009, the Academy of Motion Picture Arts and Sciences honored him as "The Michelangelo of animation."

CHAPTER 8: JOHN LOUNSBERY

John Mitchell Lounsbery was born on March 9, 1911 in Cincinnati, Ohio, but when he was five years old his family moved to Colorado. Growing up in Denver he became an active boy who loved the outdoors; in summer, the family went on vacations in the Rockies, camping and hiking, and when the snow came he turned to winter sports. This lifestyle helped spur an interest in art; sketching and painting outdoor scenes quickly became his favorite hobby.

Unfortunately, when John was thirteen, his father died unexpectedly. That left the family in a tight situation financially, and to cope with the stress he turned even more toward his art. In addition to his landscape sketches, he also began working on cartoons, finding them ideal as a way to escape the trials of real life for a while. He was a shy boy – and remained shy as an adult – but his drawings gave him a way to express himself that he was fully comfortable with. As he progressed through East Denver High School he became well known among his fellow students for his cartoons and caricatures; many of them appear in his senior high yearbook.[26]

After graduating from high school he found a job on the railways, but before too long he was able to give that up and enroll at the Art Institute of Denver. This school is gone now, replaced by the Art Institute of Colorado, but in the early 1930s, it was the place to study for any Denver artist who wanted a formal qualification. John got his diploma in 1932; he now had the credentials to start looking for a job as an illustrator, but one of his old high school friends recognized his talent and encouraged him to develop it further. Staying in school wasn't an easy choice - money was always an issue - but finally he agreed. Later the same year he moved to Los Angeles and signed up at the Art Center, a new and radical school of design and illustration staffed by working professional artists that aimed to turn out industry leaders. Even with the Depression still stifling the economy the Art Center already had a reputation; if you studied there, your chances of finding work were very high. Since it was founded in 1930, its alumni have come up with some classic art concepts, including the original "Got milk?" ads and the concept for *Star Wars* droid Artoo Detoo.[27] It worked out well for Lounsbery, too.

In 1935, one of his instructors recommended he apply to Disney, who was busy hiring to meet the demand for animated films. John figured it was worth a shot and took his portfolio down to the studio. Walt hired him right away and, thanks to his fairly extensive art education and obvious talent, didn't even start him as an inbetweener. Instead, he was immediately assigned as an assistant animator, working with Norman "Fergy" Ferguson.[28] Ferguson had no formal art training and had started at Disney as a cameraman but gradually drifted into animation work. His big break came when he designed the dog Pluto (who was named after the recently discovered dwarf planet, not the other way around). Then for *Snow White* he was tasked with the witch, and he took John onto the feature film team with him.

Once *Snow White* was done Lounsbery continued working with Ferguson, mostly on Pluto shorts. The cheerful dog was always one of his favorite characters and he was annoyed later when Ferguson's original distinctly canine style was changed for a more anthropomorphic one.

Not long after starting at Disney, John married Florence Hurd, who'd been working at another studio. The two of them settled down to a quiet, contented life on a farm and didn't get involved much in the movie industry social scene. They were content to keep Hollywood on a business footing. That worked just fine; John quickly became a star member of the animation department. After *Snow White* came *Pinocchio*, and the villains Honest John and Gideon. He animated many of their scenes, showing a distinctive style of his own and, usefully, an amazing ability to mimic the style of other animators. Soon everyone at Disney knew that John could safely be assigned to draw scenes for any character without any distracting changes in appearance. He was also outstanding at adding personality to his images, and that came across very clearly in *Pinocchio*; Honest John and Gideon are a pair who work closely together, but it's obvious right away that they're very different characters.

John also worked on *Fantasia*, drawing the alligators and hippos, and now he was working independently instead of as an assistant to Ferguson. He found it a valuable experience; because Fantasia was built around the musical pieces the animation had to be matched to the score, matching it in both tempo and mood. Everyone involved with the scene agreed he had done an amazing job of it, and Disney himself was impressed enough that only five years after joining the studio, John was promoted to directing animator for *Dumbo*. He did much of the drawing for both Dumbo and Timothy the mouse, as well as developing the structure for most of the major scenes.

Dumbo was the last major feature released before the war, and after that Lounsbery spent much of the next few years working on government contracts. One of his most important projects was *Victory Through Air Power*. Based on a popular book of the same name, this film advocated strategic bombing as a way to subdue Germany and Japan. Despite its subject, it wasn't actually an official film; Walt Disney had read Major de Seversky's book, and was so impressed at the strategic bombing concept he decided to publicize it at his own expense by making the film. Lounsbery, together with Ward Kimball, was a leading member of the animation team who turned a book of military theory into a popular film.[29] It's been controversial since the end of the war through worries it could cause offense to the Germans and Japanese. In fact, it was equally controversial when it was released because it openly supported Brigadier General Billy Mitchell, a maverick officer who'd been forced out of the US Army

in 1926 due to his advocacy of air power. Mitchell
had died in 1936 but his legacy was an uncomfortable one for the military: Mitchell had claimed that
bomb-armed aircraft could sink the US Navy's pres-
tigious battleships, and been widely ridiculed. Now
there were four shattered battleships on the seabed
at Pearl Harbor, sunk by bombs and torpedoes from
Japanese carrier aircraft; the British had lost the
battle cruiser HMS *Repulse* and the new battleship
HMS *Prince of Wales* to air attacks on the open
ocean, and the German battleship *Bismarck* had
been crippled by an air-launched torpedo, allowing
the Royal Navy to close in and sink her. As early as
1940, Fleet Air Arm torpedo bombers had damaged
the Italian battle fleet in its port at Taranto, a raid
that probably inspired the Pearl Harbor attack. It
was clear that Mitchell had been absolutely right,
and many senior officers were uncomfortable being
reminded of that. Disney didn't care; he wanted to
make a point and Lounsbery's talent helped him do
it. Watching the film now it's remarkable how the
animators managed to switch between realistic his-
torical scenes and comic segments while maintain-
ing the same high quality throughout. Lounsbery's
bold graphic style is prominent; he used a graphite
pencil for his animation sketches instead of a fine
ink pen, giving him more freedom to emphasize
lines and shading. Between him and the other animators, and Disney's determination, they created a

film that's still an excellent and enjoyable history lesson covering both aviation and the outbreak of the Second World War. The actual effects of strategic bombing – which has consistently failed to win a war then or since – are exaggerated, but that doesn't detract much from the overall effect.

With the war over and the studio switching back to its normal production, John found his talents more in demand than ever. He continued as animation director and developed characters for most of Disney's features up to *Robin Hood* in 1973. Along the way he animated many favorite characters including Donald Duck, Captain Hook and Wendy Darling, Merlin and Eeyore. His final promotion came in the early 1970s and he directed *Winnie The Pooh and Tigger Too*. He was working on his second project as a director, *The Rescuers*, when he died of a heart attack on February 13, 1976.[30] He was the first of the Nine Old Men to die.

CHAPTER 9: MARC DAVIS

Marc Davis was another boy who turned to drawing as a way to add stability to his life. He was born in Bakersfield, California on March 30, 1913, but even in a highly mobile society like the USA his parents stood out as champion nomads. The high school he graduated from was his 22nd school in almost as many towns, so it had been hard for him to form steady friendships as he grew up. His solution, whenever the family moved, was simple: until he settled in and made friends he'd pass the time by drawing, and it wasn't long before he got pretty good at it.

The Davis family wasn't wealthy, so Marc couldn't afford to go to college, but he did manage to take some art classes while they lived in northern California. Beyond that, he had to develop his skills himself and he found two places he felt comfortable doing it. One was at the library, where he could sit and sketch quietly. The other was at a local zoo. This had all sorts of advantages. He befriended zoo staff, including the assistant director, and they helped him by giving him more subjects – he was allowed in before the zoo opened to the public and animals would be brought out for him to sketch, for example.[31] Working with animals gave him a deep and intuitive understanding of their posture and movement that's very obvious in his sketches from this time.

Not long after Marc graduated high school his father died, leaving him as the only earner in the family. He picked up some jobs as an illustrator, including part-time work drawing for the now-defunct *Hollywood Citizen*. It's while he was working there that one of his colleagues told him Disney was hiring and suggested he apply for an animation job. He did, and was accepted. According to Davis "most of the applicants were unsuccessful newspaper cartoonists who didn't know anatomy. I was a newspaper cartoonist with limited success but the experiences I had at the zoo and the library made a big difference."[32]

Marc started his Disney career as an inbetweener but he didn't stay there for long. The quality of his drawings was so high that Myron "Grim" Natwick, who was animating Snow White, quickly hauled him out of the pool and made him his chief assistant. Natwick was one of the older and most experienced animators, and it was a great time for Marc. It also gave him an early insight into how differing visions could cause tension in the team; the directing animator for Snow White was Ham Luske, who wanted to portray her as an innocent young girl. Natwick wanted her to be more mature. Marc could have found himself in an awkward position, but instead he turned it to his advantage; while the senior men argued he toned down Natwick's vision to make it acceptable to Walt Disney, while avoiding the "bubblehead" character he felt Luske wanted.

After *Snow White* was released Marc was offered a job in the studio's newly formed model department, which was responsible for designing basic character concepts. It would have been an interesting job that suited him well, and working there from the beginning would have given him an opportunity to rise through the hierarchy, but he preferred to stay with animation. It was a wise choice because his next project suited his experience perfectly.

Bambi was based on a novel by Austrian theater critic Felix Salten, and the majority of the characters are animals. The decision was made that the faces of the animals would be given some slight human characteristics so they could show expressions better, but overall they would retain realistic animal shapes and movements. Marc was set to work drawing sketches and storyboards, first to develop the initial concepts and then to start laying out scenes. When Disney saw them he was stunned by the depth of knowledge that had gone into them; he immediately told Frank Thomas and Milt Kahl to give Marc additional coaching in animation so he could bring his sketches to life.

After Bambi was released Marc went back to working on storyboards, including some of the key scenes for *Victory Through Air Power* (although he wasn't credited on that). His next animation job was in 1944 working on *Song of the South*, where he drew Br'er Rabbit's first scenes and the sequence where Br'er Fox and Br'er Bear make the tar baby. The film caused some controversy when it was released in 1946; it's been described as "a jarringly inappropriate 'Uncle Tom'-ish Southern melodrama", "memorable for its utter tastelessness"[33] and even "one of Hollywood's most resiliently offensive racist texts." What nobody has ever criticized, though, is the technical quality of the animation, and Marc

Davis's work on the animal characters is regarded by many as his best.

The rest of Marc's animation career was less controversial. He continued to play a large part in designing characters, a talent that was in great demand thanks to his unbeatable knowledge of anatomy and natural movement. His abilities weren't restricted to animals, either; human characters he helped develop include Cinderella, Alice, Tinker Bell and Cruella De Vil. He wasn't entirely happy about this. The 1950s, for Marc, was a long run of working on realistic female characters, and he didn't find it much of a professional challenge. Cruella De Vil was his high point during that period; he animated every one of her scenes and thoroughly enjoyed himself with her over-the-top anger and menacing behavior.

Then he did find a challenge, from an unexpected direction. Walt Disney had been playing with the idea of a theme park since the early 1940s; he had visited many amusement parks with his daughters and was intrigued at the idea of building his own, taking themes from his films. The initial idea was to open a park beside the studios, to provide some entertainment for visiting fans. He quickly realized that the available site was far too small and expanded his ambitions. Disneyland opened near Anaheim in July 1955, and set the standard for most subsequent theme parks worldwide. Some of its biggest attractions are the famous themed rides, and Marc played a big part in making them what they are.

By this time Disney had many excellent animators, but Marc's drawing skills were more flexible than most. He could animate, but he could also produce just about any other style of drawing too, quickly and to a very high standard. His zoo-inspired grasp of anatomy and movement also made him a genius at developing characters, and the rides Disney planned were going to include a *lot* of characters. Between 1955 and 1964 Marc produced the designs for characters on nearly a dozen rides, including the classic *Pirates of the Caribbean*. His wife, Alice Estes Davis, helped out by designing some of the costumes.

Marc finally retired from Disney in 1978, but was often called back to advise and consult on various projects. Among these were Epcot Center and Disneyland Tokyo.[34] He also supported the California Institute of the Arts, which had close links with Disney. He died on January 12, 2000; that same month the Institute created a scholarship fund in his name.

CHAPTER 10: OLLIE

JOHNSTON

Oliver Martin "Ollie" Johnston was the last of the
Old Men to join Disney, but went on to become
one of the most influential. Ollie was born in Palo
Alto, California on October 31, 1912. His father was a
professor at Stanford University and Ollie more or
less grew up on the campus. From an early age, he
was fascinated by people's emotions and behavior,
and began to express his understanding of it
through drawings. He always said that at first he
was terrible at drawing and needed a lot of practice
to improve, but that may just have been modesty;
he certainly practiced a lot, but it's unlikely he was

as bad as he claimed. He did have some challenges to overcome, though. Ollie loved playing sports, but as a child his health wasn't good and he was often sick. The worst of his health problems from the point of view of drawing was palsy, which left him with tremors in his hands. He worked hard to control it, but it was a problem he suffered from throughout his life.

Although he enjoyed drawing he didn't shine in art classes at school, and none of his teachers tried to encourage him to study art at a higher level. In 1931, he enrolled at Stanford, majoring in journalism.[35] Of course, any student who wants to make the most of their time at university gets involved in other activities too; Ollie played football and ended up as the Stanford team's junior manager. He also started drawing for the *Stanford Chaparral*, where he met Frank Thomas. They made a perfect team on the campus magazine; Ollie was practical and thoughtful, whereas Frank was an experimenter who always wanted to try new styles or ideas. It worked out very well for the *Chappie* and, in the end, it worked out very well for Ollie too. If he hadn't met Frank, he said, he'd probably have graduated from Stanford and "gone to work for United Press or gotten a crummy job as an artist somewhere." Instead he finished his degree then went on to the Chouinard Art Institute in Los Angeles. There he met up with Frank again, but it wasn't long before Frank moved on to his job at Disney. Again, it was Don Graham who nudged Ollie to follow him, and after a tryout at the studio he was duly hired on January 21, 1935.

The inbetweeners pool was one common destination for new animators. Ollie got assigned to something different: he became a cleanup artist. When an animator or inbetweener draws a cel or frame, they don't actually produce the completed image that's photographed onto the film; they have far too many pictures to get done to be able to do that. Instead, what they do is draw each cel as a piece of monochrome line art. That establishes the positions for the scene, and the animator then moves on to the next one. Meanwhile, the cleanup artist tidies up the outlines if required, adds shading then colors the cel. That way, one animator can create the large number of images required for a film while simpler (but still skilled) work is done by the cleanup team. Ollie's first job was cleanup on *Mickey's Garden*. After that he worked on *Mickey's Rival*, which was animated by Clyde "Gerry" Geronimi. Geronimi was a good animator, but his personality was on the abrasive side; he was famously foulmouthed and argumentative, and most animators hated working with him; in the end, Disney sacked him after John Lounsbery fell out with him.[36] Finishing his drawings worked out well for Ollie, though. Director Wilfred Jackson called his work "the best damned cleanups" he'd ever seen. *Mickey's Rival* attracted the attention of Fred Moore, who took Ollie on as an assistant. Fred had also mentored Frank Thomas, Ward Kimball and Milt Kahl at various times; his influence and encouragement was just as helpful to Ollie. Under Moore, Ollie became lead assistant for the dwarves in *Snow White*. That was excellent experience at reconciling the different visions of Moore and Bill Tytla, the senior animator who had developed several of the characters.

After *Snow White*, Moore told Disney that Ollie was ready to work as a full animator in his own right, and he was given a Mickey short to work on. *The Brave Little Tailor* was a success, and when the team for *Pinocchio* was being assembled Disney assigned Ollie, along with Frank and Fred Moore, to animate the lead character. There could have been frustration there; Ollie had already animated several key scenes when Milt Kahl did his redesign of the character, and everything started over. In fact, when Ollie did the scenes again with the revised, less puppet-like Pinocchio, they were even better than before.

One thing that made Ollie's work stand out was his understanding of emotions and how people show them, based on his early interest at Stanford. After *Pinocchio*, he went on to animate for many classic

Disney features and some of his most remarkable scenes are those that show characters building relationships – Mowgli and Baloo in *The Jungle Book* are a great example. In fact, for any Disney feature produced right up to the beginning of the 1980s, there's a good chance that, where two characters form a team, Ollie helped with the design.

With his talents, it wasn't long before Ollie was promoted to supervising animator for *Bambi*, working together with Frank, Kahl and Larson. Again, his genius at emotions was obvious, such as the scenes where Bambi meets Faline and the Great Stag. By using gestures he was able to create believable human emotions in animals, which is not at all easy.

When America entered the war, Ollie wanted to enlist along with Frank, but the effects of his palsy meant he was classified as unfit for service. Instead he stayed at the studio throughout, working on government films as well as the shorts and features Disney was still making to boost morale. When peace – and Frank – returned he had a lot more experience to bring to his work.

In addition to his animation work Ollie was, like Ward Kimball, a huge fan of steam locomotives. Also like Ward, he didn't just like them; he collected them. In 1949, he started building a miniature railroad with three 1:12 scale steam locomotives on the grounds of his Flintridge home. He also had a country house in San Diego County with much more space around it, and there he had a mile of narrow-gauge track and a full size locomotive with carriages. It was Ollie's enthusiasm that motivated Walt Disney himself to start collecting locomotives, and in turn, inspired the railways in the Disney theme parks.

After over 43 years with Disney, Ollie finally retired in 1978. That was the start of a second career, this time as a writer. Together with Frank he wrote four books about animation and the studio, including the influential *Disney Animation: The Illusion of Life*. In 1995, they were profiled in the documentary *Frank and Ollie*, which looked back on their friendship from its beginning at Stanford.[37] They were also indirectly featured in a 1995 Mickey short, *Runaway Brain*, which starred a villain named Dr. Frankenollie. In 1999 they were voice actors in the science fiction film *The Iron Giant* and again five years later in *The Incredibles*.

Ollie was the last of the Nine Old Men. Frank died in 2004, and Ollie's wife Marie the next year. After that he retired completely, finally dying of natural causes on April 14, 2008. It was the end of a long and glorious era in American animation.

CONCLUSION

Among the thousands of animators who have
worked for Disney Studios since its early days,
what makes the Nine Old Men special? It's not just
their talent; they were all exceptionally good at
what they did, although many of them would never
have admitted it, but some truly outstanding artists
worked alongside them and never had the same influence. As well as simple ability at drawing, they
all brought something else to their jobs though –
Ollie's instinctive grasp of emotions, for example,
or Ward Kimball's gift of packing a lot of expression
into extremely simple designs. A lot of their place
in Disney history probably has to do with their ver-

satility, because in addition to drawing they could take a step up and direct or even produce a film. Then there was the way they could work together without major disagreements, especially in the case of Ollie and Frank. Their longevity as animators counts, too; many great talents came to Disney, worked there for a few years then moved on, but the Nine Old Men were in it for the long haul. Apart from those who did war service, none of them left the company once they were in. Perhaps Walt recognized that loyalty early on when he gave them their affectionate nickname.

The nine young men who joined Disney around the time of the Great Depression were able to shape the studio and its output for more than five decades, a period that covered some of its greatest successes. Even today, animators still refer to *Disney Animation: The Illusion of Life*, and while Frank and Ollie wrote it, the advice it contains draws on the skills of all of them. Without this group, there would still be a Walt Disney studio and it would still have been successful, but would it have been as successful as it actually is? Looking at the fabulous catalogue of work the Nine Old Men produced, it's hard to imagine it could have been.

[1] Disney Legends, *Ub Iwerks*
https://d23.com/ub-iwerks/

[2] *Disney's Nine Old Men: Les Clark*
https://suite.io/dominic-von-riedemann/r4427z

[3] Canemaker, John (2001), *Walt Disney's Nine Old Men and the Art of Animation*

[4] Chronology of Walt Disney's Mickey Mouse, 1930
http://www.islandnet.com/~kpolsson/mmouse/mick1930.htm

[5] Disney Legends, *Eric Larson*
https://d23.com/eric-larson/

[6] 50 Most Influential Disney Animators, *Wolfgang Reitherman*
http://50mostinfluentialdisneyanimators.word-press.com/2011/09/02/14-wolfgang-reitherman/

[7] YouTube, *Woolie Reitherman Disney Family Album Part 1*
https://www.youtube.com/watch?v=oNp7p-S3GcTM

[8] Animator Mag, *Wolfgang Reitherman remembered*
http://www.animatormag.com/archive/issue-14/issue-14-page-10/

[9] Animator Mag, *Wolfgang Reitherman remembered*
http://www.animatormag.com/archive/issue-14/issue-14-page-10/

[10] YouTube, *Woolie Reitherman Disney Family Album Part 3*
https://www.youtube.com/watch?v=llgaf6oiowU

[11] Disney Legends, *Frank Thomas*
https://d23.com/frank-thomas/

[12] 50 Most Influential Disney Animators, *Frank Thomas*
http://50mostinfluentialdisneyanimators.wordpress.com/2011/12/03/3-frank-thomas/

[13] 50 Most Influential Disney Animators, *Frank Thomas*
http://50mostinfluentialdisneyanimators.wordpress.com/2011/12/03/3-frank-thomas/

[14] IMDB, *Frank Thomas*
http://www.imdb.com/name/nm0858826/bio?ref_=nm_ov_bio_sm

[15] Disney Legends, *Ward Kimball*
https://d23.com/ward-kimball/

[16] 50 Most Influential Disney Animators, *Ward Kimball*
http://50mostinfluentialdisneyanimators.wordpress.com/2011/12/10/2-ward-kimball/

17 This Day in Disney History, *Ward Kimball*
http://thisdayindisneyhistory.homestead.com/
WardKimball.html

18 50 Most Influential Disney Animators, *Ward Kimball*
http://50mostinfluentialdisneyanimators.word-
press.com/2011/12/10/2-ward-kimball/

19 This Day in Disney History, *Ward Kimball*
http://thisdayindisneyhistory.homestead.com/
WardKimball.html

20 Cartoon brew, Dec 16, 2013, *23 Creative Christmas Cards by Disney Legend Ward Kimball*
http://www.cartoonbrew.com/wardkimball/23-cre-
ative-christmas-cards-by-disney-legend-ward-kim-
ball-92843.html

21 Disney Legends, *Ward Kimball*
https://d23.com/ward-kimball/

22 Disney Wiki, *Ward Kimball*
http://disney.wikia.com/wiki/Ward_Kimball

23 50 Most Influential Disney Animators, *Milt Kahl*
http://50mostinfluentialdisneyanimators.word-
press.com/2011/10/21/7-milt-kahl/

24 Michael Barrier.com, *Milt Kahl Interview*
http://www.michaelbarrier.com/Interviews/Kahl/
Kahl.html

[25] Disney Legends, *Milt Kahl*
https://d23.com/milt-kahl/

[26] 50 Most Influential Disney Animators, *John Lounsbery*
http://50mostinfluentialdisneyanimators.word-press.com/2011/09/17/12-john-lounsbery/

[27] Art Center College of Design
http://www.artcenter.edu/accd/about/history.jsp

[28] 50 Most Influential Disney Animators, *John Lounsbery*
http://50mostinfluentialdisneyanimators.word-press.com/2011/09/17/12-john-lounsbery/

[29] YouTube, *Walt Disney Presents: Victory Through Air Power (1943)*
https://www.youtube.com/watch?v=Nmd7Xis-flnk

[30] Disney Legends, *John Lounsbery*
https://d23.com/john-lounsbery/

[31] 50 Most Influential Disney Animators, *Marc Davis*
http://50mostinfluentialdisneyanimators.word-press.com/2011/08/20/16-marc-davis/

[32] 50 Most Influential Disney Animators, *Marc Davis*
http://50mostinfluentialdisneyanimators.word-press.com/2011/08/20/16-marc-davis/

33 The Slate Book Review, *Bristling Dixie*   http://
www.slate.com/articles/arts/books/2013/01/
song_of_the_south_disney_s_most_notorious_-
film_by_jason_sperb_reviewed.html

34 Disney Legends, *Marc Davis*
https://d23.com/marc-davis/

35 50 Most Influential Disney Animators, *Ollie Johnston*
http://50mostinfluentialdisneyanimators.word-
press.com/2011/11/04/5-ollie-johnston/

36 Blabbing on Arts and Culture, *A bit about Geronimi*
http://blabbingonartsandculture.blogspot.de/
2011/03/bit-about-geronomi.html

37 Disney Legends, *Ollie Johnstone*
https://d23.com/ollie-johnston/